W9-BWT-433

XIAOSAURUS

and Other Dinosaurs of the Dashanpu Digs in China
by Dougal Dixon

illustrated by
Steve Weston and **James Field**

PICTURE WINDOW BOOKS
Minneapolis, Minnesota

Picture Window Books
151 Good Counsel Drive
P.O. Box 669
Mankato, MN 56002-0669
877-845-8392
www.picturewindowbooks.com

Printed in the United States of America.

Library of Congress Cataloging-in-Publication Data
Dixon, Dougal.
Xiaosaurus and other dinosaurs of the Dashanpu
digs in China / by Dougal Dixon ; illustrated by Steve
Weston and James Field.
p. cm. – (Dinosaur find)
Includes index.
ISBN 978-1-4048-4718-7 (library binding)
1. Xiaosaurus—Juvenile literature. 2. Dinosaurs—
Region—Juvenile literature. 3. Paleontology—
China—Dashanpu Region—Juvenile literature.
I. Weston, Steve, ill. II.
Field, James, 1959- ill. III. Title.
QE862.O65D5963 2009
567.90951'38—dc22   2008006350

Acknowledgments
This book was produced for Picture Window Books
by Bender Richardson White, U.K.

Illustrations by James Field (pages 4–5, 7, 9, 11, 17)
and Steve Weston (cover and pages 13, 15, 19, 21).
Diagrams by Stefan Chabluk.

Photographs: BigStockphoto pages 6 (Heinz Effner),
10 (Vladimir Kondrachov), 16 (Christina DeRidder);
Frank Lane Picture Agency page 14 (Frans Lanting/
FLPA); iStockphoto pages 8 (Robert Hardholt), 12
(Chris Fourie), 18 (Andrea Krause), 20.

Consultant: John Stidworthy, Scientific Fellow of
the Zoological Society, London, and former
Lecturer in the Education Department, Natural
History Museum, London.

Types of dinosaurs

In this book, a red shape at the
top of a left-hand page shows
the animal was a meat-eater.
A green shape shows it was
a plant-eater.

Just how big—or small— were they?

Dinosaurs were many different
sizes. We have compared their
size to one of the following:

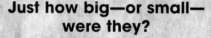

Chicken
2 feet (60 centimeters) tall
Weight 6 pounds (2.7 kilograms)

Adult person
6 feet (1.8 meters) tall
Weight 170 pounds (76.5 kg)

Elephant
10 feet (3 m) tall
Weight 12,000 pounds
(5,400 kg)

TABLE OF CONTENTS

WHAT'S INSIDE?

Dinosaurs! These dinosaurs lived in what is now the Dashanpu area in the Sichuan province of central China. Find out how they survived millions of years ago and what they have in common with today's animals.

LIFE IN CENTRAL CHINA

Dinosaurs lived between 230 million and 65 million years ago. The world did not look the same then. Much of the land was not in the same place as it is today. Early in the Age of Dinosaurs, the center of what is now China was a wide inland basin. It was full of lakes and rivers. Many different kinds of dinosaurs lived in the forests there.

The large *Omeisaurus* fed from tall branches while the smaller club-tailed *Shunosaurus* wandered by. *Gasosaurus* was too small to hunt big animals like these.

GASOSAURUS

Gasosaurus was a meat-eater that was about the size of a wolf. It had big teeth, big claws, and strong legs. *Gasosaurus* usually hunted the small plant-eating dinosaurs of the area. *Gasosaurus* often hunted in packs so it could kill much bigger animals.

Pack-hunting animals today

Modern wolves hunt in packs, like *Gasosaurus* once did. This allows them to chase and kill bigger animals such as deer.

Size Comparison

A group of *Gasosaurus* moved slowly through the forest. Soon they would come across a big plant-eater. Then they would move in for the kill.

Shunosaurus had a long neck and a club on the end of its tail. If a meat-eater attacked, *Shunosaurus* would swing the club and cause serious injury. Most long-necked plant-eaters were safe from meat-eating dinosaurs because they were too big to be attacked.

Dangerous animals today

The modern elephant is a large animal that most predators don't attack. Like *Shunosaurus'* club once did, the elephant's tusks can injure an attacker.

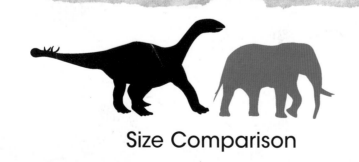

Size Comparison

A *Gasosaurus* tried to attack a *Shunosaurus*. But one blow to the neck from the *Shunosaurus'* clubbed tail was enough to stop the *Gasosaurus* in its tracks.

Omeisaurus had one of the longest necks of all of the long-necked plant-eaters. The dinosaur could reach up high and eat twigs and leaves that other animals could not reach. *Omeisaurus* often moved around in large herds.

Long necks today

The modern giraffe has a long neck. Like *Omeisaurus* once did, the giraffe can reach the highest branches.

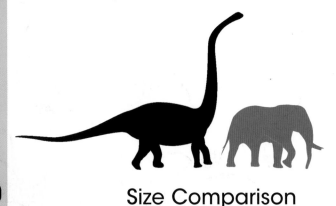

Size Comparison

An *Omeisaurus* thrust its head up to the highest branches. The dinosaur raked off the juicy leaves with its teeth. The food had a long way to go before reaching the stomach!

Not all of the plant-eaters of the region were big animals. *Xiaosaurus* was only about the size of a small deer or antelope. It fed on low-growing plants and ran on strong hind legs whenever any danger appeared.

Fast ground dwellers today

Modern meerkats keep a constant lookout, like *Xiaosaurus* did long ago. The meerkats will run away quickly if a meat-eating animal approaches.

Size Comparison

A group of *Xiaosaurus* were on guard all of the time. They knew big meat-eaters were on the prowl. If danger threatened, they stopped eating and ran for cover.

HUAYANGOSAURUS

Pronunciation:
hwi-YAN-go-SAW-rus

Huayangosaurus was a plated dinosaur. It had spikes and narrow plates that lined its back, protecting the backbone. *Huayangosaurus* had a small head and narrow mouth. It fed on low-growing plants in the forests of what is now China.

Spiky backs today

The modern tenrec has a back covered with narrow spikes. Like *Huayangosaurus'* plates once did, the tenrec's spikes protect its body.

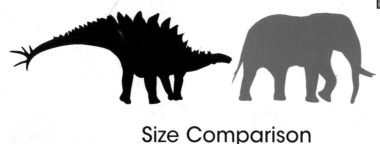

Size Comparison

With a pair of spikes and a double row of plates, *Huayangosaurus* felt safe and protected from meat-eating animals.

Hexinlusaurus

Pronunciation: HEX-in-luh-SAW-rus

The small plant-eater *Hexinlusaurus* had long legs that allowed it to run away and escape danger. But its babies were very small and easy prey. Adult *Hexinlusaurus* probably looked after their young until the babies were full-size.

Family protectors today

Modern elk live in family groups, like *Hexinlusaurus* once did. The young elk are protected by their parents until they are big enough to look after themselves.

Size Comparison

16

An adult *Hexinlusaurus* stood guard over its young. A meat-eater might have appeared at any time.

CHUANDONGOSAURUS

Pronunciation:
CHOO-an-DON-go-SAW-rus

Small meat-eaters were common in the forests of what is now China. *Chuandongosaurus* hunted for the smallest animals. The dinosaur was quick enough to hunt down fast lizards. It could also leap up to reach the pterosaurs that flew in the skies at that time.

Fast hunters today

The modern domestic cat is a small and quick hunter, like *Chuandongosaurus* once was.

Size Comparison

A pterosaur swooped down through a forest clearing, hunting for insects. A *Chuandongosaurus* leaped from the undergrowth and seized the flying reptile in mid-flight.

19

XUANHANOSAURUS

The biggest meat-eater of the ancient Chinese forests was *Xuanhanosaurus*. It hunted long-necked plant-eaters. Using strong arms and sharp teeth, *Xuanhanosaurus* grabbed the big animals and tore them apart.

Big, fierce hunters today

The modern tiger dashes out from cover to surprise its prey, just like *Xuanhanosaurus* did long ago.

Size Comparison

A *Xuanhanosaurus* was on the lookout for food. From a hiding place in the undergrowth, it saw a herd of long-necked plant-eaters. It chose a small or injured animal to attack.

Where Did They Go?

Dinosaurs are extinct, which means that none of them are alive today. Scientists study rocks and fossils to find clues about what happened to dinosaurs.

People have different explanations about what happened. Some people think a huge asteroid that hit Earth caused all sorts of climate changes, which caused the dinosaurs to die. Others think volcanic eruptions caused the climate change and that killed the dinosaurs. No one knows for sure what happened to all of the dinosaurs.

Glossary

basin—a huge hollow or depression in the land

claws—tough, usually curved fingernails or toenails

herd—a large group of animals that move, feed, and sleep together

inland—away from the shore

plates—large, flat, usually tough structures on the body

predator—an animal that hunts and eats other animals

prey—an animal that is hunted and eaten for food

reptile—a cold-blooded animal with a backbone and scales; it walks on short legs or crawls on its belly

spikes—sharp, pointed growths

To Learn More

More Books to Read

Clark, Neil, and William Lindsay. *1001 Facts About Dinosaurs.* New York: Dorling Kindersley, 2002.

Dixon, Dougal. *Dougal Dixon's Amazing Dinosaurs.* Honesdale, Penn.: Boyds Mills Press, 2007.

Holtz, Thomas R., and Michael Brett-Surman. *Jurassic Park Institute Dinosaur Field Guide.* New York: Random House, 2001.

On the Web

FactHound offers a safe, fun way to find Web sites related to topics in this book. All of the sites on FactHound have been researched by our staff.

1. Visit *www.facthound.com*

2. Type in this special code: 1404847189

3. Click on the FETCH IT button.

Your trusty FactHound will fetch the best Web sites for you!

Index

Look for other books in the Dinosaur Find series: